Pioneer
Free Will Baptists
Ministers
Burial Locations
In
California

Introduction

California

This book represents all that were part of the Free Will Baptist movement, consisting of the Palmer (south), Randall (north) and others such as the Stone, John-Thomas, John Wheeler Assns., NC OFWB and more.

Many of the photos are poor quality, but it was all I could find. Likewise, I do not have photos or tombstones for many of them. The information about these ministers were all that was available to me or found in archives. I made every effort to include those for which they would be remembered. Some I had no information, but research had shown they were of our denomination.

This Section is taken for a two Volume set done by this author.

California

Rev Blaine David Bishop
Birth:
Aug. 21, 1912
Scircleville
Clinton County, Indiana
Death:
Feb. 23, 2002
Turlock
Stanislaus County, California
Burial:
Turlock Memorial Park
Turlock
Stanislaus County
California

His name was included in the New Mexico Association as being moderator of fourth session in 1972.

Rev Francis W. Boyle
Birth:
unknown
Death:
Sep. 24, 2015
Santa Paula
Ventura County, California
Burial
Pierce Brothers Santa Paula
Cemetery

Santa Paula
Ventura County, California

Boyle served in the 526th Armored Infantry Battalion, Company B. He landed at Utah Beach in June of 1944, and fought in the Battle of the Bulge. He served two years in the Europe campaign after being deployed from Santa Paula, where he had lived on and off since he was 11 years old. Boyle was drafted in February 1943.

After stateside training Boyle's unit was sent overseas in January 1944.Boyle's unit landed on Utah Beach and then his unit worked their way through France and Belgium where they fought in the Battle of Bulge. His unit got four Battle Stars. . .they were in combat for 208 days, loss over half of our unit. He was discharged in March 1946. Post war Boyle became a Free Will Baptist minister and a Realtor/Broker. He has led 10 churches, including in Santa Paula, Boyle became a Charter Member of the WWII Memorial effort and helped in fundraising.

Francis Boyle served as Business Manager for Hillsdale FWB College in the 80's.Memorial Services was at the Santa Paula Free Will Baptist Church.

Bobby Lee Brown
Birth:
Jun. 1, 1945
Turlock,
Stanislaus County, California
Death:
Jun. 18, 1967
Modesto,
Stanislaus County, California
Burial:
Turlock Memorial Park. Turlock Stanislaus County; California,
Plot: Lot 64 Block 27

Had not long been a minister when he was stricken with a deadly disease.

Perry Delbert Buckins
Birth:
Nov. 26, 1889
Death:
Jan. 9, 1962
Burial:
Forest Lawn Memorial Park (Hollywood Hills)
Los Angeles
Los Angeles County
California, USA
Plot: Churchyard, Map B35, Lot 3455, Space 4

His name was in the list of ministers in 1937 minutes in South Carolina but did not list his state.

Rev Chester S. Burgess
Birth:
May 8, 1926
Death:
Feb. 21, 2001
Burial:
College City Cemetery
College City
Colusa County
California

An ordained Free Will Baptist minister, and active in its Calif. state work. He served on Program Committee in 1973 and was residing in College City then.
Inscription:
POPPIE PVT US Army Air Forces World War II

Rev William Halsey Callison
Birth:
Dec. 7, 1899
Missouri
Death:
Nov. 12, 1972
Yolo County, California
Burial:
Winters Cemetery
Winters
Yolo County, California
Plot: Sec 5 Lot 182 NWQ
Callison Plot

In list of Calif. State Association of Free Will Bapt. minister's deaths, in June, 1973 Minutes. He was pastor of Winters church.
Note: died in Davis, Ca 72 yrs old -Smith Chapel.

Rev Charles R. Cantrell
Birth:
1932
Death:
2005
Burial:
Oak View Memorial Park
Antioch
Contra Costa County, California

Minister/pastor for several years of Exeter, CA Free Will Bapt. church. He was active in the state and local work of his church.

Rev Daniel Clay
Birth:
Aug. 25, 1816
Buxton
York County, Maine
Death:
Mar. 18, 1907
Los Angeles
Los Angeles County, California
Burial:
Angelus Rosedale Cemetery
Los Angeles
Los Angeles County
California
Plot: Section N
Affiliated with the Free Baptists in the Northeastern U.S. A bio sketch states he ministered mostly in San Pedro, CA.

William E. B. Condit
Birth:
May 1, 1924
Locust Grove
Mayes County, Oklahoma
Death:
Jun. 24, 2013
Pryor
Mayes County, Oklahoma

Burial:
Cherokee Memorial Park
Lodi
San Joaquin County, California

Dr. William E. B. Condit was born to W. C. Pigeon (Ross) Condit. E. B. graduated from Locust Grove High School in 1943. He furthered his education at Northeastern State College where he graduated in 1953 with a degree in Industrial Arts. He finished his education by obtaining his Doctor of Theology while living in Sacramento, CA. E. B. served his country proudly in the United States Navy from October 1, 1943 until January 11, 1946. On July 5, 1946, Mary Louise Littlefield and William E.B. Condit were united in marriage. This began a marriage of 67 years that coupled raising a family in the ministry, pastoring churches from North Carolina to California, ministering for over 64 years. On Aug. 1, 1949 Condit was ordained to preach as a Free Will Baptist Minister. In 1949 he organized the Little Rock Free Will Baptist Church east of Locust Grove where he was their first pastor. He then spent 1 year at Lowry Free Will Baptist Church before organizing Trinity Free Will Baptist Church in Muskogee. After 3 years there, E.B. was the pastor at Free Will Baptist Churches in Wewoka, OK, Bakersfield, CA, Ponca City, OK, Modesto, CA, Campbell, CA,

Concord, CA, Ontario, CA, Farmville, NC, back to Campbell, CA, and Lompoc, CA. He also served as interim pastor for home missions at many churches in between. E.B. served on the California State Mission Board as well as the California Christian College Board for 17 years. Many pastors and Christian leaders were born from E.B.s ministry throughout the years. Before moving back to OK, they lived in Lodi, CA. Their ministry in California spanned over 38 years. He and his wife moved back to Mayes County, OK in 1998 where they lived west of Pryor. He remained an honorary member of Capital Free Will Baptist Church in Sacramento, CA. He always put God first. He also treasured the time he spent with his family provided a great fatherly image for his children grandchildren to follow. Every two months, his family would receive a hand written encouraging message from him. E.B. loved to watch football. He was a avid Oklahoma Sooner Football fan! He was also a fan of the San Francisco 49ers. E.B. was very patriotic was known to write governmental dignitaries to share what he believed to be right. For 5 years, E.B. played guitar sang in a family quartet that shared in song preaching by broadcasting at KOLS radio in Pryor. He was also a founding member of the original Cherokee Ramblers Band. E.B.'s life serves as an example to follow his ministry will flourish for many generations to come. Reverend Adrian Condit and Reverend Larry Condit officiated.

Grover Morley CONDLEY
BIRTH
6 May 1896
DEATH
20 Feb 1959 (aged 62)
BURIAL
Reedley Cemetery
Reedley, Fresno County,
California

An early Free Will Baptist minister, who served in AR in early years. Arkansas WW I Veteran. Thank you for your service.

Osmondo Corrales
Birth:
Dec. 4, 1921
Pinar del Rio, Cuba
Death:
Mar. 7, 2013
Culver City
Los Angeles County, California
Burial:
Inglewood Park Cemetery
Inglewood
Los Angeles County, California

Osmundo Corrales was born in the small community of El Sábalo located in the Pinar del Rio province of Cuba.

His parents, Cerbellon Corrales Yut and Rosa Blanco Menéndez, were excellent examples and guided him well in his life especially in the areas of respect, honor and interpersonal relations. He was the next to the last among eight siblings: Antonio, Eusebia, Luz Maria, Josefina, Andrea, Cándido, Osmundo and Magdalena.

He embraced the Gospel of Jesus Christ during the decade of the 40's when he was 19 years old. In October 1941 he was baptized by immersion in a strong flowing river by Rev. Luis Díaz. In October 1944 he enrolled in the Free Will Baptist Seminary, "Cedros Del Libano". During the summer of 1947 he was called as interim pastor of the church in the small town of Arcos de Canasí, in the Province of Matanzas. He later returned to the Seminary in the fall of 1948 to continue his Seminary studies. He received his graduation degree from the Seminary in 1950. One year later, May 16, 1951, he was ordained as a minister of the Gospel with the laying on of hands of the presbytery of the Seminary where he graduated and where they were celebrating the National Convention. In the fall of 1945, Osmundo met a young lady that had come to enroll as a student in the Seminary. For 62 years Celia was his faithful companion in the ministry which he had chosen in obedience to God's calling. From Osmundo and Celia's marriage were born two children, a daughter, Omayda and a son, Omar. Corrales was pastor of several churches: Free Will Baptist, Viñales, provincial de Pinar Del Rio, Cuba, Free Will Baptist, La Lisa – Marianao, Cuba. Free Will Baptist Church, Bryan, Texas; Resurrection Free Will Baptist Church, Culver City, California. Brother Corrales was a living example of love for God. He has left a void in the pews of his church and in the hearts of all of his brothers and sisters in Christ, which will only be filled when we too are in the presence of our glorious Savior.

Luther R Crumb
Birth:
1891
Death:
1973
Burial:
North Kern Cemetery, Delano, Kern County, California

He began preaching in the many rural churches found in eastern OK. Where he was ordained is unknown, but was enumerated in old minutes of the Free Will Baptist Association of churches and was an active minister. Sometime after 1940, removed to central California, where he again, preached and carried on with church work, while working to provide for his family. During a time when he stopped to help a motorist, a fire ensued, burned his arm so badly, it was amputated from the elbow down. For sure, this was a great loss, but after some recovery, he went on working with one hand. He preached, attended meetings, until health prevented it.

Grover Morley Condley
BIRTH
6 May 1896
DEATH
20 Feb 1959 (aged 62)
BURIAL
Reedley Cemetery
Reedley, Fresno County,
California
In memory of an early Free Will
Baptist minister, who served in
AR in early years. Arkansas WW
I Veteran. Thank you for your
service.

Native of Arkansas, he had lived
in Turlock since 1979. He was a
pastor in Arizona, Oklahoma,
Arkansas, and in California at
Hughson and Modesto. He
served on various boards and
committees during his successful
ministry.

Orbin Hurst Doss
Birth:
Feb. 28, 1912,
Arkansas
Death:
Dec. 28, 1985,
Stanislaus County,
California
Burial:
Turlock Memorial Park,
Turlock,
Stanislaus County,
California,
Plot: Lot 233 Block 28

Israel Bunyan Dunaway
Birth:
Apr. 7, 1884,
Hartselle,
Morgan County, Alabama
Death:
Mar. 30, 1960,
Fresno County, California
Burial:
Mountain View Cemetery,
Fresno, Fresno County,
California.
He was an ordained minister of
the Free Will Baptist Church, and
was elected moderator of the
Eastern Association of Oklahoma
in March of 1940. He was one of
the founders. It is believed he
came from the Texas West Fork
Association to Oklahoma,
probably from Eastland, where
his family is shown in the census.
His name was in records and old
news items in the Ada Weekly of
Pontotoc, Oklahoma. At what
point he moved to California is
not known. He was probably a bi-
vocational minister as many
were in his time.

Dr Aristide T Ferguson
Birth:
1851
Death:
1935
Burial:
Forest Lawn Memorial Park
Glendale
Los Angeles County
California
Plot: Gardenia Terrace, Great
Mausoleum, Columbarium of
Protection, Niche 12211

Rev. Aristide T., son of William J. and Caroline (Heitgeberg), was born on the Island of Guernsey, England, Oct. 1, 1859. He studied at his native place and at Moody's School, Northfield, Mass. He was converted in 1870. In 1885 he did the work of an evangelist in Chicago. After two years he became pastor at

Bulver, P.Q., where he was ordained June 19, 1887. In 1888 he moved to La Grange, ME, and has also under his care the churches at Milo and Medford Centre. He has been commission agent in France two years, mineralogist in California and Arizona, and cashier in Chicago. In 1888 he married Miss Nellie Turville.

Rev Horace Graves
Birth:
Sep. 27, 1834
Guilford
Piscataquis County, Maine
Death:
May 5, 1912
California,
Burial:
Woodlawn Memorial Park
Compton
Los Angeles County, California
Plot: Section S, Lot 34, Grave 1S

He became a Christian at the age of nineteen and was a student in Bangor Theological Seminary one term. His license to preach was granted in March 1859, and in June 1863, he ws ordained at South Dover, ME., by a council of the Sebec Quarterly Meeting (Q.M.)

His pastorates have been at South Dover, Atkinson, Bradford, East Bangor, Dover, and Springfield (1887).

In the last two places he has had revivals, and also in Bradford, where he organized the church. He married Miss Sarah A. Magoon, of Dover, ME, and has five children living.

Claudie Hames
Birth:
Nov. 22, 1925,
Kellyville,
Creek County, Oklahoma
Death:
Mar. 9, 2011,
Bakersfield,
Kern County, California
Burial:
Hillcrest Memorial Park,
Bakersfield,
Kern County, California

He attended schools in Sapulpa and started working at an early age at Liberty Glass Co. He joined the 503rd Regimental Combat Paratroop Division of the Army on February 10, 1944, to serve his country during World War II.

He served on Lyte, Corregidor and Negros, in the Philippine Islands. While on the Island of Corregidor, he was wounded by shrapnel with injuries to the spine. He was temporarily paralyzed and spent 59 days in the hospital before returning to battle. He was a recipient of the Purple Heart. He returned to Oklahoma and relocated to Taft to work in the oilfields after the war. He worked for Rocky Mountain Drilling Co. On May 13, 1953, he accepted the Lord as his Savior. Mr. Hames accepted the call to preach the Gospel of Christ, and within a few months accepted the pastorate of the Lamont Free Will Baptist Church. He moved to Oxnard, California to pastor the Oxnard Free Will Baptist Church, a position he held for eight years before his move to Bakersfield in July 1964 to pastor the First Free Will Baptist Church. He pastored this church until his retirement in 2001. He also served on the National Home Mission Board of Free Will Baptists during this pastorate. His greatest joy in life was door-knocking, asking people to come and visit the church, and leading someone to the Lord.

Alfred C Hogbin
Birth:
May 9, 1846
Buckland
Kent, England
Death:
Sep. 20, 1920
Los Angeles County
California
Burial:
Forest Lawn Memorial Park
Glendale
Los Angeles County, California
Plot: Azalia Terrace
Great Mausoleum
Azalia Columbarium, Niche 28

Alfred C. Hogbin was born in Buckland, Kent, England and came to American when his family immigrated to Wisconsin about 1855. He was the oldest of John and Mary's sons who survived into adulthood. On Feb 21, 1865, he enlisted as a Corporal in Company D, Wisconsin 49th Inf. Reg. and mustered out on November 1 1865. Later in his life, he was active in the GAR.

He graduated from Hillsdale College in 1872 and Harvard Divinity in 1875. He had two other brothers that were graduates of Hillsdale College who were FWB ministers. George and Richard Lawrence who had changed their name for an unknown reason. In 1876, he married Flora Preston (Hillsdale class of 1876). He and his wife traveled extensively. In addition to his ministerial work, he was a published author.

He served as a pastor in New York City prior to going to Sabatha, Kansas where he served for twenty-one years. He then served as pastor for eight years in Laramie, Wyoming.

He and his wife went to Europe in 1916 where he studied modern language and history. They were at the University of Grenoble in France when World War I broke out. He remained in France until 1919, when they returned to Hollywood, California.

Truman Niece Huddleston
Birth:
Jan. 19, 1910
Hartshorne, Pittsburg County,
Oklahoma
Death:
Sep. 8, 2004
Olympia, Thurston County,
Washington
Burial:
Chowchilla Cemetery
Chowchilla,
Madera County, California
Rev. Huddleston's parents were William Adam Huddleston and Nancy Belle (Allen) Huddleston. She died in 1918, when Truman was a child. His father remarried to Beulah Alice (unk) Huddleston, and both died in California. Truman N. Huddleston was ordained a Free Will Baptist minister when he was 35 years of age at the FWB Church at Non, OK. He was active in the church's ministry, and in the Center Ass'n meetings. He married Isadele and they removed to California in the 1940's. He lived at Chowchilla for years and held pastorates in the area.

William Adams "Bill"
Huddleston
BIRTH
11 Aug 1876
Pontotoc County, Oklahoma,
USA
DEATH
tf4 Apr 1972 (aged 95)
Madera County, California, USA
BURIAL
Golden Sunset Memorial Park
Kerman, Fresno County,
California

Prior to his marriage to Beulah Alice Ward, William was married to Nancy Belle "Nannie" Allen (b. 1887 in AK.d.1918 in OK) on Oct 23, 1901 in Oklahoma. He may have been married prior to that as well but unable to find a record however, 1940 US Census lists William's son Albert (his last child with Nancy) as living in Compton, CA with his brother Henry Huddleston born in 1897.

Note: The birth year on the marker is incorrect according to his World War I Draft Registration Card and his Social Security Death Notice. He was born in 1876 not 1873

He was a minister in the Freewill Bapt. church...I believe he carried credentials. His son, Truman, was also a minister, ordained in OK, and carried on pastoral work in Calif.

Rev Ansel H Huling
Birth:
Jun. 7, 1838
New Berlin
Chenango County, New York
Death:
Sep. 4, 1917
Los Angeles County,
California
Burial:
Forest Lawn Memorial Park
Glendale
Los Angeles County, California
Plot: Section H, Map 1,
Lot 120, Space 8

An ordained Free Baptist minister/pastor, editor and writer. From NY, where his father, Rev. Daniel Huling, was a Freewill Bapt. for 35 yrs. After Daniel's death, the family moved west, to OH, Mich, Wis, Neb, and to Calif. Rev. Ansel H. Huling, son of the Rev. Daniel and Lydia (Burlingame) Huling. He was educated at Mendota Seminary and Hillsdale College.[Mich]. His ordination took place in 1863. He has held pastorates at Sugar Grove, Ill, Raymond and Evansville, Wis. He was one of the founders of the Christian Freeman and was one of its editors and corporators. In 1874 he was chosen editor and manager of the Western Department of the *Morning Star.* He was instrumental, as agent of the Wisconsin Yearly Meeting, in the founding of the Cairo, Ill. Mission. He has been several times elected delegate to General Conference, and has been a member of the Home Mission Board. He was married in April, 1860, to Emily L. Stewart. His home is in Cincinnati, where he is engaged in literary work."

John Jay Hull
Birth:
May 31, 1847
Death:
Aug. 8, 1933
Burial:
Chrome Cemetery
Chrome
Glenn County,
California

An ordained FWB minister who labored in Wisconsin churches and with his father in South Dakota.

Rev William Cheney Hulse
Birth: 1839
Ohio
Death: 1920
California
Burial:
Bellevue Memorial Park
Ontario
San Bernardino County
California
Plot: E-054-02

HULSE, Rev. Wm. Cheney, 1839-1920; b. OH, d. Calif; He was bn in Medina, OH, and lived in 1879, in Wis, for a dau was born there to him and his wife, Marilla (Douglas) Hulse. There is a link to a previous wife, but I've found no record of that marriage. He and Marilla share a stone with its pic on the memorial.
Family links: Parents:
 Lester Orista Hulse (1813 - 1893)
 Hannah Cheney Hulse (1812 - 1886)
 Spouses:
 Esther Chase Hulse (1842 - 1876)
 Marilla Douglas Hulse (1850 - 1928)*

Rev Jesse L. Jeffrey
Birth:
Jun. 23, 1913
Ellis County, Texas
Death:
Feb. 27, 1984
Colusa County, California
Burial:
Oak View Memorial Park
Antioch
Contra Costa CountyCalifornia

First moderator of the Arkansas State Association of FW Baptists. His name is listed in "Hist. of Free Will Baptist State Associations," Edited by Dr. Robt. E. Picirilli, in 1976. Parents: John Jesse Welch Jeffrey and Lena Wilma (Anderson) Jeffrey.

Edward "Butch" Johns
Birth:
May 7, 1924
Death:
Oct. 20, 2010
Burial:
Shafter Memorial Park
Shafter,
Kern County,
California

Edward "Butch" Johns, U.S. Veteran, who was faithful to the Free Will Baptist denomination serving as preacher and church planter for 60 years.

Paul Kennedy
Birth:
Apr. 4, 1921
Quinton, Oklahoma
Death:
Aug. 6, 2009
Tulsa, Tulsa County, Oklahoma
Burial:
Sunset View,
Amador County, California

Paul Kennedy was an active layman in California serving as a state leader and Promotional Director. Paul was a generous man and shared his rare book denominational collection to the Historical Archives at Hillsdale College, Moore, OK,

Rev Benjamin Franklin Kelley
Birth:
Nov. 11, 1832
Middlebury
Wyoming County, New York
Death:
Jan. 29, 1914
Santa Cruz
Santa Cruz County, California
Burial:
Santa Cruz Memorial Park
Santa Cruz
Santa Cruz County, California
Plot: Block D, Lot 33

Ordained Freewill Baptist minister in 1859 from NY; went West and ministered in Minn-Wis. and organized churches there. He also occupied the office of town treasurer. On Jan. 1, 1887, he resigned the pastorate of the Delavan (Wis.)

He organized the Free Baptist Church in Madelia, MN, on 27 Mar 1875. Later he held a state-wide position with the Baptist Church.

Married: Charlotte Adelia Douglas about 1852 in Plainfield, Wisconsin. They had at least 6 children: Laura, Lucetta, Angelena "Annie", Mary, Emeline "Emma", and Viola. Charlotte died on 11 May 1886.

Married: Missouri A. Connor on 18 Nov 1886 in Watonwan County, MN. She was born in 1840 in Indiana. Her parents were Alexander and Louisa (Reavis) Connor. With Benjamin, she appears on the 1895 Minnesota census, living in Rockford, MN. No further information (death/burial) has been found for her.

Married: Frances A. "Fannie" Blood on 18 Oct 1898 in Madelia, MN. She had previously been married to Manilius Snow and had 5 sons with him; he died in 1898. She died in 1918.

Free Will Baptist ordained minister, pastor and leader. He was the California State Executive-Secretary of California FWB's and editor of *"Voice"*. He was manager of the state bookstore.

Winston Benton Lawless
Birth:
Feb. 1, 1913
Death:
May 30, 1986
Burial:
Clovis Cemetery,
Clovis,
Fresno County, California

Raymond Earl Letsinger
Birth:
Aug. 17, 1902
Death:
Sep. 12, 1983
Burial:
Hillcrest Cemetery
Porterville
Tulare County, California,
Plot: M-1770-2

A Free Will Bapt. minister, whose name is in list of 1961 State roll of ministers. His address was Porterville at that time.

Archie J. Mayhew

Birth:
May 10, 1926,
Saint Cloud,
Stearns County, Minnesota
Death:
Oct. 26, 1997,
Modesto,
Stanislaus County, California
Burial:
Lakewood Memorial Park,
Hughson,
Stanislaus County, California

The Rev. Mayhew lived in Modesto for 32 years and for his past six years served the Free Will congregation. Previously, he spent more than 17 years as a missionary in Ivory Coast, West Africa. According to his wife, "The Lord called him to go to Ivory Coast and that's where he was happiest. Most of the work was village work. We would go and teach in the villages." Rev. Mayhew lived in Modesto from the time he was 12. He served in the Navy during World War II.

Doice Lee McAlister

Birth:
Oct. 23, 1929
Pottawatomie County
Oklahoma
Death:
Apr. 27, 2010
Turlock,
Stanislaus County, California
Burial:
San Joaquin Valley National
Cemetery,
Santa Nella Village,
Merced County, California

He was the pastor of Tulock Free Will Baptist church for about 35 yrs. He preached for about 60 yrs. He was great brother and and good pastor and many people loved him. He had over 400 people at his funeral service in the church.

Inscription:
US ARMY Note: KOREA

Rev J. L. McAlister
Birth:
Sep. 29, 1924
Hector
Pope County, Arkansas
Death:
Oct. 23, 2013
Farmersville
Tulare County, California
Burial:
Exeter District Cemetery
Exeter
Tulare County, California

He was the youngest of five brothers and five sisters. J.L. was educated in Hector, Arkansas and later earned his Associate of Arts degree at California Christian College. On August 19, 1950, he married Wilma Juanita Rodgers and they enjoyed 63 happy years of marriage. After becoming a Christian at the age of 40, J.L. spent the rest of his life telling people about Jesus. He pastored Free Will Baptist churches in Lindsay, Farmersville, Earlimart, Visalia and Exeter for 35 years. He served as a mentor to many young preachers. He lived his life to the fullest. His favorite place to be was church. He enjoyed spending time with his family, gardening, shelling and selling walnuts and, most of all, visiting people.
Rev. J. L. McAlister was 89.
Published in Visalia Times-Delta and Tulare Adv-Register on Oct. 25, 2013

George W McLain
Birth:
Jun. 6, 1894,
Oklahoma
Death:
Jan., 1965,
Fresno County, California
Burial:
Odd Fellows Cemetery, Fresno,
Fresno County,
California

Rev. McLain was a pioneer minister in the state of Oklahoma and known for his successful evangelism and as a church planter. Rev. McLain was of Choctaw Indian descent, of which he was proud. He as a young man, worked closely with Rev. Elzie Yandell, an older minister, in eastern Oklahoma, who mentored him and held revival services with him. He was a motivator wherever he pastored. He often went to a church that was in a low state, and brought it to vitality and on successful financial footing. A son, Joy McLain, was elected delegate to the General

Cooperative Ass'n. Meeting in Denison, TX in 1934. When the State Ass'n met in Ada, OK; he was elected as Okla. State Evangelist in 1936, along with Dr. I.W. Yandell and Rev. Paul Purcell. In 1941, as state evangelist, he reported having eight revivals, 249 conversions, and organized three churches the past year. He was active in the state work, and often called upon to preach in their meetings. Rev. McLain pastored Ada First FWB in Oklahoma before moving to California, and then the Richmond First and Selma, churches.

Rev William V. McPhail
BIRTH
30 Sep 1907
DEATH
6 Jul 1969 (aged 61)
BURIAL
West Side District Cemetery
Taft, Kern County, California

William V. McPhail, pastor of the Free Will Baptist Church in Taft,

Rev Joe L Mooneyham
Birth:
1916
Mississippi
Death:
Feb. 24, 2001
Ceres
Stanislaus County
California
Burial:
Cremated,
Specifically: unknown

Rev. Mooneyham, 85, died in a fire that consumed his home at las Casitas mobile home.
An ordained Free Will Baptist minister/pastor for 55 years in California's San Joaquin Valley.
The Rev. Brown, state director of ministries of the Free Will Baptist Church, will led funeral service.
Rev Mooneyham Founded Village Chapel in 1957 and served 10 years before resigning because of health from related to muscular dystrophy. A church building, Mooneyham Hall, was named after him.
Rev. Mooneyham next worked briefly as a cook at the California Bible Institute in Fresno before returning to Modesto in 1969 to serve as visitation Minister at Prescott Bible Church in Modesto (now Prescott Evangelical Free Church.). He led a Spanish-language congregation at one point and did missionary work in Central America.
He led churches in Visalia and Tulare befor moving Stanislaus County. Family members say he served in the ministry 55 years.

Walter Stanley Mooneyham
Birth:
Jan. 14, 1926
Houston,
Chickasaw County, Mississippi
Death:
Jun. 3, 1991
Los Angeles,
Los Angeles County, California
Burial:
Desert Memorial Park,
Cathedral City,
Riverside County,
California,
Plot: b-30,264

Dr. W. Mooneyham joined the U.S. Navy and served in the Pacific Theater (1943-45). He received his Bachelor of Science degree in journalism at Oklahoma Baptist University, Shawnee, Oklahoma (1950) while ministering as pastor at First Free Will Baptist Church, Sulphur, Oklahoma (1949-53). After working with the National Association of Free Will Baptists in Nashville, Tennessee (1954), he became Director of Information (1959) and Interim

Executive Director of the National Assn. Of Evangelicals in Wheaton, Illinois (1964).

As a special assistant to Billy Graham, he coordinated the World Congress on Evangelism in Berlin (1966). One year later, he was appointed Vice-President of International Relations for the Billy Graham Evangelistic Association. From 1969 to 1982, he was the President of World Vision Intl., a service agency providing childcare, emergency relief assistance and mission's research to Christian denominations in over 30 countries.

He was the recipient of three honorary doctorates: Houghton College, New York (1964), Taylor University, Indiana (1977) and Seattle Pacific University, Washington (1978). Dr. Mooneyham hosted and appeared in many television documentaries and prime-time specials such as *Come Walk the World*, a weekly documentary about Christian missions, and a weekly program, *Larry Jones Presents*, that he produced and which was aired on 200 stations. In 1980, he was the subject of a prime-time documentary about the refugee Vietnamese "boat people" who he helped rescue at sea.

He was the author of eight books and of innumerable magazine articles. His latest book was *Dancing on the Strait and Narrow* from Harper and Row, 1989.

He holds many honors such as the Polish Orthodox Church's Order of Mary Magdalene for extraordinary service to children and the Republic of Korea's highest award to foreigners, the Distinguished Service Award.

George N. Musgrove
Birth:
December 10, 1855
Kings County,
New Brunswick,
Canada
Death:
1924
Burial:
Evergreen Cemetery
Los Angeles
Los Angeles County, California
Plot: Section I

He was converted when 19 years of age. He would was a student for the ministry ever made theological Seminary, received his licensed to preach on December 1, 1879 and was ordained February 20, 1883 by Rev. Louis mild learned, EM. Eight. Quimby and others he held

a few churches in New Hampshire before accepting the call to the Arlington church in Rhode Island.

Roy E. Pembrook
Birth:
Aug. 28, 1917
Death:
Dec. 10, 1993
Burial:
Westwood Hills Memorial Park
Placerville
El Dorado County, California

Plot: Parkcreek 74-A4-181 He was a retired minister at the time of His death at age 76. He was converted at age 12 and began to preach at age 15. He was ordained in Missouri on August 17, 1934 at the Mountain Grove FWB church. A native of Watson, Missouri he preached in various churches and held revivals in the state. After moving to California, he served on the Executive Committee and helped organize new churches. He organized or pastored the Martinez, Brentwoods, Antioch and Pleasant Hill churches.

John Lee Reel
Birth:
Jun. 7, 1905
Appleton
Pope County, Arkansas
Death:
Jul. 10, 1989
Visalia
Tulare County, California
Burial:
Visalia Public Cemetery
Visalia
Tulare County, California
Plot: Sect. A, Blk 16, Lot 15,
C/E Grave

His parents were James c. Reel, and Josephine (Prince) Reel. He married Elsie Violet "Vi" Eakin, Oct. 25, 1924, in Pope Co. AR. They had four children: .It was after 1940 census that John and Violet moved to Oklahoma, around the Tulsa area. He

became an ordained Free Will Baptist minister, and later moved to California, where he pastored the Visalia FWB Church, and others. He was active in his district association of churches, serving on boards, and was a good pastor.

Tip Richardson
Birth:
Sep. 16, 1923
Norwood, Wright County, Missouri
Death:
Mar. 3, 2013
Tulare County, California
Burial:
Visalia Public Cemetery

Visalia, Tulare County, California Tip was born to Arthur and Dora Richardson. He married the former Nina Kelley in Norwood, Missouri on December 6, 1942. Tip served in the navy during World War II as a dental assistant. In later years, he retired from Tulare County Family Support Division. He served as a minister of the Free Will Baptist Church in various valley locations. He was known for his love of singing and did so until he became ill. He left behind his wife of 70 years, Nina. (Published in Visalia Times-Delta and Tulare Adv-Register on March 6, 2013)

Rev Charles P Roam
Birth:
Apr. 18, 1941
Death:
Dec. 21, 2015
California
Burial:
Floral Memorial Park,
Selma
Fresno County, California

He was a Pastor of Grace Free Will Baptist Church, Selma, CA, at the time of his death. He had been pastor in other churches in the state during the previous years. He was active in his church's enterprises.

J L Roler
Birth:
Jan. 23, 1845
Racine, Ohio
Death:
Apr. 5, 1939
Burial:
Lindsay-Strathmore Cemetery
Lindsay
Tulare County, California

He was converted in January, 1866 and received his license to preach 10 years later. He was ordained in November, 1884. He was pastor of the Third Alexander and Lodi churches in South East Ohio. He was clerk of the Athens Quarterly Meeting. On March 11, 1869 he married to Alvira Smith.

Rev Daniel Joshua Rowlett
Birth:
Apr. 21, 1901
Dutton
Madison County, Arkansas

Death:
Oct. 21, 1964
Exeter, Tulare County, California
Burial:
Exeter District Cemetery
Exeter, Tulare County, California

Rev. Daniel Joshua Rowlett son of John Anderson Rowlett (1874-1950) and Polly Weatherby (1883-1927). Married to Maudie Rae Phillips on 30 Oct 1925. Children: Daniel Joshua Rowlett Jr. (1927-1967) and Wesley Eugene Rowlett (1929-1981).
In list of Calif. ministers for the State Association of FWB in 1961.

Rev Tom I. Rowlett
Birth: 1904
Death: 1984
Burial:
Visalia Public Cemetery
Visalia
Tulare County
California
Plot: Sec. F, Track 2,
Tier 8, Grave 81

Ministered to churches in Calif. FWBapt.

Sheldon J. Smith
Birth:
Apr. 14, 1836
Elbridge
Onondaga County, New York
Death:
May, 1914
California
Burial:
Woodland Cemetery, Woodland,
Yolo County, California
Plot: Blk-17 Lt-31 Gr-15

Son of Bliss and Priscilla (Rounds) SMITH, was married to Miss Emily Hakes Feb. 14, 1856. In 1882 she died, and he afterwards married Miss Susan Stevens. In September 1873. He was ordained by the Church of God. In 1885 he united with the Free Baptists, and pastored of the church at Corey Hill, Van Buren County, Mich. In 1882 he was elected department chaplain of the G.A.R. of the state of Michigan, having served in the late civil war in a New York Regiment." He moved from Michigan to Yolo Co. CA, where in 1910 census, he was living alone at age 74.

Rev Olney M Temple
Birth: Jul. 25, 1872
Tuscarawas County
Ohio
Death: Sep. 25, 1964
Alameda County
California
Burial:
Harmony Grove Cemetery
Lockeford
San Joaquin County
California, USA
GPS (lat/lon): 38.14796, -121.17778

TEMPLE, Rev. O.M. (Olney Monson), b. 1873 OH; d. 1964, Santa Clara, CA; His parents were Joseph Nixon TEMPLE, and Sarah E; 1880 Cambridge, OH, Census, with parents plus sibs: Olney 8y OH; Iona M, 5y, OH; and Clyde B, dau, 3y OH.
Married to Jessie Emma (James) Temple, 30 Nov. 1892, Tuscararas, OH;
In Wisconsin 1905 Marcellon, Columbia Co. Wis. w/3 kids; In 1920 Los Angeles, CA census, occ: pastor/church, with three children, James B., 25, Grace E b. IL, 15y, (b.12

Oct 1904), and Gladys M, b. Wis Apr. 14, 1907.
In his early years, he served as a minister in the Freewill Baptist church in Wisconsin until it merged with the American Baptist in 1911; then he continued as a minister/pastor in Calif.

John Alexander Logan Waltman
Birth:
Dec. 13, 1886
Kirbyville,
Taney County, Missouri
Death:
Dec. 11, 1959
Turlock
Stanislaus County,
California
Burial:
Turlock Memorial Park
Turlock,
Stanislaus County,
California

He was married to Livia Elizabeth (Graham) sometime after he arrived in Oklahoma from Missouri, before 1910. They lived in Oklahoma for some years where their children were born. Shortly after 1940, they moved to central Calif., where Rev. Waltman began the Turlock Free Will Baptist Church March 22, 1942, with nineteen charter members. He was elected its first pastor. In the following months lots were purchased and in 1945, a new church auditorium was built at Landers and "C: streets. The church worshiped there for almost twenty years. Rev. Waltman was pastor from 1942-1946. He was active in the state work. He was a member of Turlock at the time of his death at 73 years lacking three days being 74 years. ---info from HISTORICAL CORNER, of the *"Voice"*, official organ of the State Assn of Free Will Baptists.

Rev Jerry Dale Watson
Birth:
Jan. 11, 1935
Sulphur
Murray County, Oklahoma
Death:
Dec. 29, 2003
Fresno
Fresno County, California
Burial:
Visalia Public Cemetery
Visalia
Tulare County, California

An ordained Free Will Baptist minister, and pastor. He served on the Calif. FWB State Mission Board in 1973, and later, and other offices. He was active, and esteemed by all who knew him. Jerry married Betty Lois Cooley in Visalia, Calif. December 28, 1955. He was born and raised in Sulphur and graduated from Sulphur High School in 1953, where he was active in sports and in the agricultural program. Jerry moved to California in 1955. He attended the College of Sequoias, California Christian College in Fresno and Pacific Bible University in Fresno. He was ordained in 1961 and served as Pastor for the Freewill Baptist Church for 42 years in the Visalia and Fresno areas. He retired from pastor ship in August of 1988. He was employed by Miller Memorial Chapel as Funeral Director for over 25 years, continuing his ministry to families and co-workers.

Services for Pastor Jerry was at the Miller Memorial Chapel in Visalia, Calif. with Rev. Tim Rolen officiating.

Rev John Jay Weage

Birth:
1831
Cattaraugus County, New York
Death:
1898
California
Burial:
La Vista Memorial Park
National City
San Diego County, California

Rev. John Jay WEAGE, son of Ira and Keziah (Darling) WEAGE, was born in Cattaraugus Co. N.Y., in 1830. He received a license to preach in the Free Will Baptist Church in 1855 and was ordained by the Honey Creek Quarterly Meeting (Wis), in 1863. He was five years principal of Prairie City Academy, Illinois, and has held pastorates at Raymond, Wis., St. Albans, Paloma, Fairview, Wheatland, Curnes and Kawanee, Illinois, also six years with congregational churches, and later ministered to the church at Smyrna, NY.

He was married to Mary C. Dudley, daughter of Rev. D. Dudley, 19 Nov. 1856, Warren, OH.

Rev Morris Armstead Wood

BIRTH
11 Jun 1895
Arkansas, USA
DEATH
8 Sep 1968 (aged 73)
Fowler, Fresno County,
California, USA
BURIAL
Woodlake District Cemetery
Woodlake, Tulare County,
California, USA

Morris A. Wood, 73, a long-time minister in the San Joqauin Valley, died in a Fowler hospital. He was a resident of Woodlake where he retired two years ago. A native of Flippin, Ark., he moved with his family as a small boy to Oklahoma where he was reared. He served in the U.S. Army during World War I. On June 28, 1922, Mr. Wood married the former Zola Holmes in Pauls Valley, Okla. He had been a pastor for 54 years and spent 35 of those years in the San Joaquin Valley, holding pastorates in Stockton, Sultana, Raisin City, Riverbank, Fresno, and Woodlake. He had two brothers who were also free will Baptist preachers namely; Rev. Vard

Wood of Stratford, Okla., and Rev. F.M. Wood of Ada, Okla

James Clinton Wood
Birth:
Oct. 25, 1928
Oklahoma
Death:
Dec. 14, 200
Fresno, Fresno County,
California
Burial:
Clovis Cemetery, Clovis,
Fresno County, California

James Clinton Wood's parents were Walter F. and Hallie Wood. He was an ordained Free Will Baptist minister and pastor, pastoring at Salinas and Tulare, CA.

James M. Woodman
Birth:
Feb. 12, 1824,
Tamworth, Carroll County,
New Hampshire
Death:
Dec. 27, 1903,
San Leandro,
Alameda County, California
Burial:
Chico Cemetery, Chico,
Butte County,
California

He united with the Free Will Baptist church in Sanbornton when fifteen years of age, and the following year was in preparatory studies of theology with Rev. J. Woodman at Lowell, Mass. He then studied at the Dracut Biblical School in Dracut, Mass, traveled as an evangelist two years and was ordained in 1844 at Limerick, Maine. He entered the Biblical School at Whitestown, N.Y., in 1845, and graduated two years later. He later attended the Botanico Medical College in Cincinnati, Ohio where he received a medical degree May 15, 1848. After preaching a short time at South Parsonfield and at North Berwick, Maine, he went West for his health and ministered to the Honey Creek, Wisconsin church during 1850-56, and the Mt. Pleasant church 1856-61, when in 1862 he went to California, where he has been principal of the Chico Academy. Sometime prior to 1866, Rev. Woodman erected a building for use as Mrs. Woodman's private school. On Nov. 12, 1874, the building was destroyed by fire, evidently the work of arsonists. The Academy was rebuilt and in 1884-5, the academy listed Rev. James M. Woodman, principal, his wife, Selena, ass't principal; his son, Charles, teacher. In 1897 Rev. Woodman formally retired from active preaching and built a new home in San Leandro, CA. He is author of *"God in Nature and Revelation," "The Song of Cosmology;" "The Neptunian Theory of Creation* "and other articles for newspapers in Boston and Chicago.

Arvel Earl Woolery
Birth:
Feb. 14, 1912
Oklahoma
Death:
Jun. 20, 1982
Lindsay, Tulare County, California
Burial: Hillcrest Cemetery, Porterville, Tulare County, California
Plot: Z-86-4

Woolery was a WW II Army veteran, enlisting 30 Oct. 1943 at Fresno, and mustered out, 09 Jan. 1946. After his service, he became a bi-vocational, ordained Free Will Baptist minister. He worked at different jobs that allowed him to have flexible time. He retired from the Kern Co. School District, in the 1970's. He became pastor of Selma Church, Porterville for several years, then at Earlimart for about a decade. Each place saw progress under his leadership.

Rev. Woolery was a kind and generous man, soft spoken, and he usually thought before he spoke. His wisdom was useful to many of his peers and friends.

Joseph Elzie Yandell
Birth:
Feb. 5, 1880
Scott County, Arkansas
Death:
Jan. 23, 1970
Burial:
Clovis Cemetery
Clovis
Fresno County, California

He was ordained at Lodi (Latimer County Oklahoma) to preach for the Free Will Baptist Church in 1904. He farmed as most ministers did during this time, and went far and near to preach. He baptized probably more people in eastern minister of his day. He organized churches, held revivals, funerals and weddings, and was in demand as a speaker wherever he went. In 1929 he took his family to California. He was in the organization of the Oklahoma

State Association of Free Will Baptists, at Holdenville, Oklahoma in 1908, where he was elected moderator, and his brother, Dr. I.W. Yandell, clerk. He had a serious demeanor, a good head, and was known for his honesty. He had an active life of faith and preaching for over 67 years. His memorial service was held in the Chapel of California Christian College, Fresno, with Dr. Wade T. Jernigan, officiating.